Things That Keep and

Do Not Change

BY SUSAN MUSGRAVE

POETRY

Songs of the Sea-Witch 1970
Entrance of the Celebrant 1972
Grave-Dirt and Selected Strawberries 1973
The Impstone 1976
Selected Strawberries and Other Poems 1977
Becky Swan's Book 1977
Kiskatinaw Songs (with Seán Virgo) 1979
A Man to Marry, A Man to Bury 1979
Tarts and Muggers: Poems New and Selected 1982
Cocktails at the Mausoleum 1985
The Embalmer's Art: Poems New and Selected 1991
Forcing the Narcissus 1994
Things That Keep and Do Not Change 1999

FICTION
The Charcoal Burners 1980
The Dancing Chicken 1987

FOR CHILDREN
Gullband (Illustrated by Rikki) 1974
Hag Head (Illustrated by Carol Evans) 1980
Kestrel and Leonardo (Illustrated by Linda Rogers) 1990
Dreams Are More Real Than Bathtubs
(Illustrated by Marie-Louise Gay) 1998

NON-FICTION
Great Musgrave 1989
Musgrave Landing: Musings on the Writing Life 1994

COMPILED AND EDITED
Clear-Cut Words: Writers for Clayoquot 1993
*Because You Loved Being a Stranger: 55 Poets Celebrate
Patrick Lane* 1994

Things That Keep and
Do Not Change

SUSAN MUSGRAVE

Canadian Cataloguing in Publication Data

Musgrave, Susan, date.
    Things that keep and do not change

Poems.
ISBN 0-7710-6676-7

I. Title.

PS8576.U7T44 1999   C811'.54   C99-930052-0
PR9199.3.M87T44 1999

We acknowledge the financial support of the Government of Canada through the Book Publishing Industry Development Program for our publishing activities. We further acknowledge the support of the Canada Council for the Arts and the Ontario Arts Council for our publishing program.

Typeset in Fournier by M&S, Toronto

Printed and bound in Canada

McClelland & Stewart Inc.
The Canadian Publishers
481 University Avenue
Toronto, Ontario
M5G 2E9

    2 3 4 5   03 02 01 00

to my daughters,
Charlotte and Sophie

my friends
Patrick and Lorna

and for Stephen

CONTENTS

Part One: The Laughter in the Kitchen

Part Two: Do Not Make Loon Soup

ONE

The Laughter in the Kitchen

The legless man in the motel room next to me
listens to country and western music
all night, an endless song
about going down on his knees
for some faithless woman's love.
I turn in my bed, thinking of you the day
we thought our daughter had gone
missing. The moment
before she disappeared you'd seen a stranger
on the block, the kind who wore
a stained suit from the Sally Ann, the kind
who couldn't know innocence
existed. Our daughter was supposed to be

next door, playing in the fenced yard
with two neighbour boys. You'd been
on the phone and I'd turned my back
on the moment to do something
predictable – move the garden sprinkler,
open the morning mail – acts
that would never again seem so ordinary
once we'd made up our minds
between burial or cremation. Your body

had never felt so alive as you took off
in the car, driving down

every back lane, listening for her
glove-muffled cries. You drove

deeper and deeper into the kind of hell
we reserve for ourselves and never want
our children to have to know. You knew

at this moment she could only be suffering
in the hands of that stranger who would afterwards
stuff her trusting body into a single forest
green Glad Bag, then tote her to the park.

They would find her legs first, dangling
from the swing, shoes on the wrong feet
as usual, arms hanging from the jungle
gym. I'd want to touch, to straighten
her turned-in toes: how clumsily
we lived on this earth!

She was lost only for a moment, locked
in a spare bedroom with the two boys
next door, not wanting her privacy interrupted,
but in that moment when she was gone
forever, death in all his beautiful variety
sang to us, off-key and aching
inside our cheated hearts.

All day our daughter and her best friend
have been playing marriage, destroying
the house to make it the way they need it
to be. They've shoved the loveseat
across the bedroom door to form a barricade,
overturned the armchairs to give themselves
temporary shelters. They've even rolled
the carpet back, "so the carpet won't get
beer spilled on it," my daughter, pretending
to be Dad, explains, when I complain:
the house doesn't feel like my own any more
but still I have to live in it. "We can

build a new house when I make lots of good
money," my daughter says, butting out
the Popeye candy cigarette she won
from the neighbour boy for showing him
her vagina through a slit in the split
cedar fence. I wept, told her next time,

baby, hold out for a whole pack,
trying to be brave, the way only a mother
could. "We can't build anything if you
keep drinking drugs," the tiny wife bursts
as my daughter keels into the cookstove
and pretends to catch fire, the laughter

in the kitchen filling the house
where we tried to live. What has become

of my young life, the man who once pressed
a fistful of crocuses between my breasts
and made love to me on the kitchen floor
while beyond, on the river,
a loudspeaker-toting paddleboat carried
honeymooners to the mouth. Later we took
the same cruise, pretending to be newlyweds
ourselves, holding hands on the tipping deck
with others who took photographs to prove
they had truly been there, they had
loved each other – once. The laughter

in the kitchen reminds me: grief
is a burden, something to be shaken
like the foxgloves in our garden, stooping
under the weight of their seeds. I've learned
the lessons of pain, now wait for the same
light that makes my daughter's face so
luminous and wise as she says to her small friend,
"Now you be Dad. You've got no body so you can't
get away. I'll be the mother this time."

Your mother sang lullabies to send you
early into the underworld. You remember
waking in a dream, your mother cradling
your head. Your first words were unintelligible
to anyone but her, she knew from the start
you said, *I want everything*. You're still
the same, you've lived that way, wanting
even more. And now your mother
is dead. The boy you once were
picks up the pistol he last fired
the night your father was shot
in the head, the boy you'll always be
fires at his lonely reflection and weeps
when the mirror does not break. This
is your power. To prepare for death
and send people you love into that other
place. So it was when your mother sang
don't say a word, preparing you for sleep.
How did it, so soon, become morning?

Sailing south up the north coast
of Labrador, tired of photographing whales,
icebergs – *All nature is but art unknown*
to thee – tired of my imagining self, I go
back to my cabin and read – *All chance,*
direction, which thou canst not see. One poem
sticks: a boy, Eddie, naked under a tree,
tiny penis bleeding from someone's switch,
the same person who has taken photographs
and left the yellow film boxes littered
around the boy's feet. The poem is entitled

"A Violation." Over lunch I discuss
mind-body unity with two Buddhists
from Winnipeg, how each juncture of the healing
journey presents us with a choice, a turning
point – whether to split off
from our experiences or make what has happened
part of our Becoming. I'm struggling

with this, back on deck trying to photograph
a whale breaching, but I'm never quick
enough. I return to my quarters, defeated
by nature and technology. And unable to forget
the violation of Eddie Trainor. It reminds me
of the beating my own brother took, barely six,
my father expected him to act

like a man. The bully, an older boy,
straddled my brother and punched him until
his knuckles were raw and my brother's face
a blur of crushed flesh and gracelessness.
Then my father berated him for being weak,
the loser. I believe my brother
split off from himself that day –
And spite of pride, in erring
reason's spite – it was a turning
point in the process of his Becoming
insane. My women friends joke about men being
so insane they won't ever stop
to ask for directions, they always have to
prove themselves and can't get it up any longer
even if you tell them you've got all night.

One truth is clear: whatever is, is right.
Then I remember my two boys as I was
going out the door, my frail sons becoming
fierce, always fighting in those days
over which would be the first one
to kiss his mother good night.

When I was old enough I dug
the eyes from my mother's china doll
and buried them on a beach.
No one could reach me with small
talk of sadness after that: my tears
became the property of Mother-May-I
who always answered, "No-you-may-not."

When I was mad enough I tore the doll's
real hair out by the roots until
my own skull looked like a cool zero with two
holes, a nose and a mouth. No one spoke
of choice as I sat cramped in the back
of the Buick with my mother sighing
how she'd looked at life from both sides
of the same two bits, and my father
threatening to drive the car off
the biggest bluff if she didn't quit.

On the last birthday my mother gave me
a bottomless cup. I felt the first tears strike
my face, gather in the dim mouths
of my eyes as she sat blaming me for her
guttering light. I was her poison
she said, the potion she could count on

when it came to sacrificing love. But by then
I thought only of returning it, unable
to bear the debt of it, this gift
she called my life.

In Spanish prisons the "water cure"
was used to determine innocence,
the prisoner bound, mouth held open
by a sharp-edged prong. A strip of linen
conducted water into the mouth,
like a stream like the swollen stream
you have chosen to picnic beside, wiping
clean the faces of your young children
with cool linen smelling of warm fruit
and later, in the hottest part of the day,
watching them strip and plunge, breathless,
into the water, each one determined to stay
under the longest *causing the victim to strangle*
and choke. You look up from your book, almost
loving the way your children can hurt you,
their sharp-edged joy.

"Time to get out of the water!" you cry
as they disappear a final time, their innocent
mouths opening then closing. You watch them break
from the surface choking, "no no we don't
want to go now, not yet." But you know you have
already outlived your children as they dive
and scream in your bloodstream slipping away.

THE NOISE A SKELETON MAKES
TRYING ON A NEW BODY

At night in the hospital, far
from the dark shore your body washed
up on, I hear water lapping
under a becalmed hull, your lungs still
gulping air, then releasing it. Grief
is a voyeur here, peeping from the nest
of wild birds outside the barred window
in the pear tree that will never bear,
at least not this time around.
I stroke your thin hands, kiss
the track marks along your arms,
the veins that took me somewhere
I never intended to go. At first

the sound is indistinguishable
from the rest, the noise your body makes
trying to laugh, feel, sit up in bed
as our daughter arranges cream-coloured
freesias in the blue vase beside your head
and John, the Irishman, lights
a contraband cigarette. At first
I am resigned, I have been getting used
to the future. But then I begin to believe
you'll do it, this time you'll get better
forever again, one day

we might even be able to talk
without raising our voices. What
would we hear each other say
as our daughter turns the flowers so they
too can get a good view of the room
and what lies beyond? Our daughter

who looks like you. She says she can
smell and taste and hear everything,
especially your sadness. Sometimes
your sadness hurts her ears. To show you
how much, she puts her hands over her ears
then lays her trembling fingers on your face
as if they can still give you the power
to heal. Now your hands flail towards her
grace like birds first entering the sky
they've so often failed to reach.

MUTE SWANS

All winter you stared into the deep harbour
where, that last summer, our two children
drowned. You wore a red shirt to their service,
though red was never a colour I'd associated,
until then, with mourning. But you had always
refused to mourn or inhabit your body
until you filled it again with enough heroin
to make it safe. Our daughters were buried

in a common grave under a shade tree
chosen for its shallow roots. I believe
we held hands while we picked the grave,
at least allowed our fingertips to touch,
before I walked back alone to serve tea
and the lifeless cakes a grieving neighbour
had provided. The coffin seemed so plain,
whiter than the mute swans our eldest daughter
had painted last spring before your hands
began to shake and the world became
the colour of bruised veins. I try

to remember the immense beauty of pain,
the boat shimmering red like the rush
of blood you sucked up every hour
into a syringe. The children were too far
out, too young to know anything

about drowning, and you so unable to lift
your arms to save them. We buried them

wearing identical dresses even though
in life I'd never dressed them in anything
the same. I let someone else choose,
a specialist who said white was the most
innocuous colour, the one least likely
to incite strong emotion. My friends
thought I had no feelings because I couldn't
weep, not even when the red boat
was hauled to the surface of the green water
with its limp cargo, and those small
bodies full of choked water lay wrung out
on the beach. I gave up feeling, what use

would it have been to feel? At night
when you nodded off by the window
I took turns in their twin beds, turning down
the covers as if they still might move
over and make room for me. On the wall
above the beds, the unfinished watercolour;
I remember our eldest daughter
making her young sister pose, a sheet
draped over her teetering body, her white
wings closed. After the death

it was your stillness I could not bear,
the way you sat waiting,

as if you expected two mute swans to alight
upon our world, our life, and give us
light in darkness. Sorrow is nothing.
Small things keep us safe.

when we arrived, only my father's house
in a stony pasture, and a crucifix
nailed to a stunted medlar

to hex the snakes, hundreds of them,
who slipped their way out of the dark earth
to bathe under the shedding sun; I was the kind
of kid who could whup a snake from here
to kingdom come: that was my father's

expression, from here to kingdom come.

When you've had your father's blood
on your face, how can you write about it?
When you walk around in the hat
he shot his head off in, what can you write?

I loved his brown eyes, his voice,
the scent of his pipe tobacco
like wildflower honey mixed with wind.
I imagined the smell of the honeysuckle
he promised to plant each fall
as if anything could take hold in that place
and grow. The night he left he told me
next year I will plant my best garden ever.
And I knew, like all the other mysteries
of his life, it would exclude me. I can still see

the way he pulled the brim of that hat down
over his eyes. And I still hear those snakes
in the black hold of this earth, plotting their own
garden where they could crawl from here
to kingdom come, trying to understand
what it took to be a man.

Remembering her bad dream, my daughter
wants to let the fish go. This is the same
fish that whispered to her in her sleep,
warned her, "You have seen God, seen him
lead you towards the river, felt the knife
that was meant for me." We tried
to comfort her, took her fishing as if to prove
God would not send us anything
we could not bear. I carried the knife
to clean the fish afterwards, though she cried
to hold it, to show us she could be so careful.

Her father wanted her to bait a hook,
but she flinched and turned from him
because a hook had to hurt, it had to
hurt in the parts of the body raw
sunlight never reaches.

When the fish struck her father lifted it,
gold in the flashing morning, and our daughter
pleaded with him to let the fish go. She said
a silver fish would be luckier, it would glint
in the shallows like a dipped knife:
let the gold carp go, take his bad luck back
to where mysteries remained unexplainable.

We didn't know better; we hurried
the body to higher ground and laid it out
under the sun where it seemed to sigh,
as if wishing it could have been silver, luckier.

We didn't know what to do, and in that
moment when the gold carp held us wavering
in its eyes, my daughter seized the knife away
and plunged towards the certainty of the river.

We put her body into the ground.
It's taken me a lifetime to say
we put her body in the ground
and the ground wept. We believed
we found forgiveness in the earth's
grief, in the shock of wet dirt we dug
through before striking those tumbling
roots. There's no marker, nothing to say
her trusting naked body lies in peace. Only
a mound just out of reach under the nettles
and wild peppermint. We slipped her body
into the ground the way she squeezed herself
into the shining blue leotards she lived in.
She was so alive, exquisitely unaware
of her own existence as she cartwheeled
across the heavens, somersaulting
into the star-struck universe.
How small death seemed in her spinning sky.
How true the sound of our weeping.

TWO

Do Not Make Loon Soup

and bread by the woodstove
waiting to be punched down again.
I step out into the dark
morning, find the last white flowers
in a Mason jar by the door
and a note from a friend saying
he would call again later. I go back
into the kitchen, tomatoes
on the windowsill after rain,
small things but vast
if you desire them.

The deep fresh red.
This life rushing towards me.

THE SITUATION IN WHICH WE ARE BOTH AMATEURS
for Bill Hoffer (1944–1997)

I came to you last night and we tried
to talk – how you were beginning to consider
the virtues of death, how dying would be just
like you, we should consider your absence
your gift. You held your breath, trying not to
cough – *there I go, having symptoms*
in front of you – while we sat
in the wind-raked garden
where the patio door kept banging open
and almost-shut. Neither of us got up,
unable to admit it distracted us
from the situation in which
we are both terrible amateurs. You said
I've had a pretty good life
for a guy like me. Growing up at all
was a bloody miracle. You said, *Please don't*
be unhappy about me, and the door
banged shut.

It's as if you'd gone out
to bury a seed and that seed
had come back to you, promising
more than it once was. Only I bury you
for colder reasons, none
of them having to do with death.

You wished for madness
but your wounds were never deep.
You need to take your grief
backwards into the depths, let it
drink of that element from which
so much life has sprung.

DESIRELESS: TOM YORK (1940–1988)

I had said there would be no more poetry
for friends dead, or friends dying

I had said that but when the call came
and I heard your name, and said your name
back again over the impossible long distance,
my ear pressed hard against the black receiver,

I knew poetry would come back. It had to.
Because, Tom, I see you driving alive
down that dark Arkansas road the moment before
your old car is accordioned into something else
impossible, the radio still playing
a tune you could tap your foot to

as you drive. And in your eyes
for the moment something glorious
comes through. Even in that moment, Tom,
something glorious comes.

A FRIEND WRITES TO THANK ME
FOR CHINESE WILLOW USED IN
THE ART OF JAPANESE FLOWER ARRANGING

Mutilating and bending the green stems,
how you cut them for me
where I might bend, also, and allow
my own body to be flayed, the raised flesh
under my fingers today in some ways
like binding feet or boarding up
an infant's head: beauty here,
beauty there. I've known men
go faint with passion over hair
on the legs of a woman, others breathless
over a pierced nipple, a stretched neck.
Who's to say. Thanks again, anyway.

SEX AFTER SIXTY
for Peter Gzowski

That got your attention,
didn't it? Or maybe you've lost interest
and moved on to another poem, one
about the ecstasy of a rousing foursome
of bridge, the *Tropic of Capricorn* as a hot
topic for literacy, or the cool seduction
of the golf course on a July day, plums
buzzing with bright wasps, young girls
making daisy chains in the grass, the scent
of vanilla bourbon on the breeze

but I digress. This was to be about sex
after sixty. The Inuit have 85 words
for sex between the ages of forty-five
and fifty, after that there gets to be less
and less until it fizzles out, down
to one word maybe, "later." It still happens
though, as John Berryman, sexagenarian, said,
you sit by fires when you are young
and when you're old you do the same, only then
you do it more slowly. But there's hope, look

on the wild side, Leonard Cohen
turns sixty this year also
and is famous for not only his big
poetry but his ever-increasing sex

appeal. In one of the most passionate
exchanges of my career to date, Leonard
wrote to me only last week, asking, "Can you
send me a photograph of Peter G?"

For some, sixty is just
a beginning, when the heart starts to come
on, and you move in close, hold on
to that microphone so that women everywhere
sigh at your composed voice, about to break
the news that you are not quitting, not
this year, not yet. By the way, when you
think of it can you remember to send
that photograph for Leonard C? I picture you
posed against ageless bricks, a wreath
of cigarette smoke around your face, smiling
for eternity, waiting for the click.

HOLY GROUND

for Arlene Lampert

We left the literary party Al Purdy
had invited us to in some sad-luck Toronto
hotel, picking our way over the drunks who had fallen
asleep on the stairwell, through the ladies
of negotiable virtue outside. You made me
hold your hand, you in your mini leather coat,
me an innocent from the Queen Charlotte Islands
in my flowing gown and the Irish widow's shawl
I always wore back then as if I had looked
into the future and seen what was in store.

We made a pair! Old laughing girls we dubbed
ourselves Wardey Birdsong and Blossom Endrott
for the evening, imagining for the moment
what it felt like to be wholly desirable.

I wanted to look them in the eyes, these hungry
men under the All-You-Can-Eat Pizza signs:
I'd thought of men as our allies.
Don't look at them, you hissed, gripping
my hand harder. Instead of cutting through
the unlit lot to our car you said we would skirt
the whole block. Neither of us knew this was Hog Town's
Holy Ground; we trudged the oldest known gauntlet
of sneers and solicitations, non-literary
invitations we pretended we didn't understand.

"If you won't fuck us," they cried, "fuck you!"
Oh, Wardey, I whispered, *what should we do?*

You always knew what to do. And that's how
I still think of you, strutting way up ahead,
defiant, no shame on you. You always knew
where we were headed, too,
didn't you?

DO NOT MAKE LOON SOUP
(Valuable Advice from *The Eskimo Cookbook*)

For a week I'd been struggling to write
a poem about Canadian unity; not an original word
had come to mind, only Brendan Behan's reminder
that an author's first duty is to let his country down.

On Saturday night I invited a few friends, poets
like me feeling the torpor of the unemployed, for a potluck
dinner. Joe Rosenblatt brought the entree, a loon fresh
from Qualicum Beach; true Canadians, we were all too
reserved to ask under what circumstances did he acquire

this fresh loon, what became of its life-partner, and so on
and so forth and that and around. I suggested we cook
the loon straightaway; Lorna Crozier said,
but we don't have a recipe,
as Pat Lane plucked the feathers off with his teeth
then cleaned the bird and tossed it in my stockpot with water
to taste. *Don't hold back on the salt,* cried Lorna,
it's the spices that make all the difference.
Al Purdy opened a homemade beer
and poured it into the soup, a little *je ne sais quoi*
for flavour. I told them, then, how I was stuck
on a poem about Canadian unity, could they help me
out? No help came. *Canadian unity,* said Al, eventually,
isn't that some kinda oxymoron? Joe said,

Even our new coins are separating. Wherever you look
there's symbolism.

Pat, the patriot, began reading American poetry
to the morose carcass in the stockpot, convinced,
I guess, a dead loon would be more
of an audience than four stuck poets after a few drinks.
He read "13 Ways of Looking at a Blackbird"
and as he read I decided to retaliate
(with apologies to Wallace Stevens):

    Eleven Ways of Looking at Canadian Unity

    I
    Among twenty Rocky mountains,
    The only moving thing
    Was the loon's eye opening and closing
    In the poet's stockpot.

    II
    I was of three or more minds
    Like a country
    In which there are two or more distinct societies.

    III
    The loon simmered in its watery kettle,
    a small symbol of national unity
    and fairly well cooked.

IV

Quebec and the rest of Canada
Should be one.
Quebec and the rest of Canada and a cooked loon
Should be, too.

V

I do not know how to compare
The beauty of Quebec
To the beauty of the rest of Canada,
The loon before he is cooked
Or just after.

VI

The shadow of the loon
lolling in boiling water creates
a restless mood across the nation.

VII

O politicians of Canada,
Why do you put loons on our coins?
Do you not see how the loon
Sinks to the bottom of this stockpot;
That it's hard for citizens to scrape off
The stuck bits?

VIII

I know Canadian regional accents,
Bilingualism and the *patois* of Montreal
But I know, too,

That the loon is involved
At almost every level of government.

IX
When the loon flew into the telegraph wire
At Qualicum Beach, the poet recognized it
As being one of many cliches.

X
At the sight of the loon
In a stockpot far from home
Even the bards of southern Vancouver Island
Would cry out in both official languages.

XI
It was Canada. Snowing.
Beer was flowing and you could
Count on it, there would be
More demonstrations, more
Unemployed poets. The loon
simmered in a paltry bit of
oversalted water all evening.

Just as I finished, Lorna, still looking for a recipe, found
The Eskimo Cookbook. Never cook a loon, it advised.
Do not make loon soup, but suggested boiling a fresh
snowy owl instead.

As I dished up the loon I realized our mistake:
the flesh was stringy, fishy-tasting, tough,

and there wasn't very much of it, hardly enough
to go around. Nevertheless we choked it down
then strolled out under the budding maple
to the beach where the sun was going down
reminding me once again of my duty as a writer
to let my country down. Then, out above the water
I heard a lonely cry – it sounded like O, Canada! –
from sea to sea-blue loon-filled sky.

1: How Portable My Pain

On New Year's Day my love went away
and left me with nothing
but the poems of Paul Durcan.
There are worse things a man can do
than leave a woman alone
with the poems of Paul Durcan.

I read, and wept, then read some more
and pretty soon I had fallen in love
with the enormously lonely selected
poems of Paul Durcan.

And as I took a train from the west
out of Ballinasloe later that evening
with a pocket full of earth-smelling
potatoes I'd purchased as a gift
for the poet in his lonely Ringsend bedsit,
the signs were all around: Wrinkles Beauty
Salon, Nutter's Bar & Spirits, Wacker's
Pet Shop, UP IRA — I knew I was on my way
into the centre of the universe
of a poem by Paul Durcan. I could picture
myself tapping at his small door
in the calm centre of the universe,

not knowing what I would have to say
if only he ever answered. I tell you

when I got there I found a note
banged to that door saying sorry for leaving me
stranded, he might be across the road consoling
the jilted neighbour whose lover had run off
with a blonde telephonist from Ulster leaving her
with six highly illegitimate children

or he could be down the street calming
the good woman Mrs. Murphy whose husband practises
self-exposure in front of the television leaving her with
feelings of self-recrimination

or possibly he was up the way placating
the recently widowed beauty whose husband
had torched her wardrobe: by now

I had begun to realize it was by no means
a simple thing to be sucked into the whirlpool
at the centre of the universe
of a poem by Paul Durcan. My head was full

of interrogation marks, I won't deny, and oh,
I don't know, I stood there, my pocket full
of those dark earth-smelling potatoes, which I
considered leaving on his doorstep
in the shape of the ultimate interrogation mark

all the while telling myself there are worse things,
yes, far worse things a man can leave a woman with
than the selected poems of Paul Durcan.

I lost the keys to the car
on the strand at Slyne Head.
I had put the keys in my windbreaker
pocket that had a hole in it
without thinking because I had been
thinking about the poems of Paul Durcan.

I found a round stone with a hole in it
while thinking about the poems of Paul Durcan.
The hole in the stone didn't go
all the way through, not like the hole
in the pocket of my windbreaker did go
all the way through: I lost that lucky

stone, also, and I was a long way from home.
Just then I felt like writing the world's loneliest
poems but Paul Durcan had already written them
and I was travelling with my mother, anyway,
who hates the wind. This is what she says
to me, she says, "I hate the wind." I wanted
to say to her how can you *hate* the wind
but I could tell she had made up her mind
about it already. And that was that.

I lost the keys to the car, the car
to the keys, Registration number DS VF263
and my mother hated the wind. On the strand

at Slyne Head I put the car in my windbreaker
pocket that had a hole in it
without thinking because I had been
thinking about the poems of Paul Durcan.

In Clifden I lay in bed with Paul Durcan
and his selected poems, in bed wearing nothing
but my white flannelette nightie
with what looks like chicken parts all over it,
thinking of him in his bed wearing nothing
but the women's pyjamas he bought
thinking they were men's pyjamas
at Marks and Spencer's in Dublin.
If I had known his number
I would have telephoned to describe
the scent of cock
and hen grilling, a scent that filled my head
as I read, much out of breath, his selected
poetry. I was unable to detect the source
of that scent, checked under my spare
pillow, searched under the bed. I even
sniffed the pages of his book and then

there we were, standing together on the Old Bog
Road between Murvey and Ballyconneely, me
wearing nothing but my white flannelette nightie
with what looks like chicken parts all over it,
and you in the women's pyjamas you bought thinking
they were men's pyjamas in Dublin.

My mother spent her morning searching
the room for a pair of black
woollen socks she bought yesterday
in Westport. I could have stayed
in bed forever reading the selected poems
of Paul Durcan but my mother's sighing
made me anxious, and I got out of bed, placed
his open book on the table next
to my nerve-pill collection
and started to take a breath. It was then
I noticed a few page numbers in his book
had gone missing, and, when I looked further,
the title had disappeared, also. Paul,
what has become of you? Don't leave me alone
on this road to Sligo with my barefoot
mother weeping for some wool socks
she bought yesterday in Westport while I climbed
into the black hills with nothing but your book
between my breasts and the wind. I prefer that
nakedness to how I am now, driving the grieving
road to Sligo with nothing but a pair
of black socks, inside out, blinding my eyes.

After the Cliffs of Moher we took the road
inland to have tea and cheese toasties
at Kilfenora. Even though my mother
was tired I read her the poem I had written
to my father, who, when the time came,
wouldn't fit in his coffin. "I suppose
it's lovely," she told me, "and probably true.
But I don't understand a word of it."

Later, in an Ennistymon guest house
while my mother rested, I found, in the selected
poems of Paul Durcan, a poem where his mother
said she did not comprehend a word of his new
book, the poems he had composed to *his* dead father.

I wanted to read my mother this poem, too,
and say, look, Mum, Paul's mother feels the same
as you. But I didn't. Not yet. Instead
I took her back to the black
coast of Doolin and Doonbeg where the water,
black, was the colour of my father's
dying light. Black, black. You, Paul,
of all, might understand that.

Because I feared Aer Lingus
Flight 374 would explode in mid-air
en route from Shannon to London
over the Irish Sea, I took on board
with me the selected poems of Paul Durcan.
That way I would have something to cling
on to, something to clutch that would forever be
a comfort to me, with Mr. Garvey, in the seat
next to me, an explosives expert on his way
to London to deliver a lecture, and my mother
in the aisle seat, set to go off. When he wasn't defusing
bombs, so to speak, Mr. Garvey
said, he spent his time writing
verse, specifically about terrorism
and generally about agricultural practices
in Ireland during the famine,
most of which were bleak. Mr. Garvey knew,
too, many of the poems
of Paul Durcan, having been privileged
to memorize them during his term at Mullingar
Mental Hospital. As we dipped
over the Irish Sea he said he'd always feared
the resurgence of his insanity, would I let him
wear my copy of the selected poems
of Paul Durcan on his knee, or, better still,
around his neck as a kind of oxygen mask
or a life jacket? This is how I came to part

with my solitary copy of the selected poems
of Paul Durcan. I felt considerably ill
at ease until we landed at London's Heathrow
where Mr. Garvey wanted to know would I
accompany him to dinner and an old film
starring Mickey Rourke in Leicester Square,
the one where he blows up
a schoolbus full of innocent schoolchildren.
Only Mr. Garvey called them "*so-called* innocent
schoolchildren" and for that he was not
allowed to leave the plane, nor, as far as I know,
board any other, not ever. I left him
sitting there, Row 3, Seat B, the poems
of Paul Durcan open on his knee. "Strange bird,"
my mother said, as we boarded our Canadian
flight, the one that would carry us on home
after a brief stop to refuel in Calgary.
When the hot meal was served somewhere
over Reykjavik my mother poked around
in it, and seemed pleased. "I'm glad
this chicken doesn't have a bone," she said.
"I wondered how I was going to cope."

MACBETH'S GHOST IN THE ENDIVE
In memory of George MacBeth

We had been out of touch, ever
since his death he had not written so much
as a postcard from Scotland saying never
before he was sixty had he picked up
a prostitute or written a hexameter,
a combination he felt likely to prove

fruitful. Later I missed his letters
about the bog road he could see from the hospital
where tinkers had lighted fires
for the solstice the day his first
daughter was born. And then the last
letter with the grave
news of his health, postmarked Ballyruin.

But finally you appeared to me, George,
in the form of a bit of endive concealed
amongst the lettuce, avocado, and tomato
of my salad. You went down the wrong way,
as my mother used to say, and I fled
the table choking, to the mortification
of my companion, a British travel writer,
who had just dropped your name.

I was so sure it was you, George, that I
pressed that shred of retched-up endive

in my Day-at-a-Glance where I scribbled
this poem. I've always remembered
your birthday and even though you've ceased
writing back, today is no exception.
January 19, 1996, your 64th. I hope some
smoking hooker lights a Gauloise for you
afterwards as you toss off a quick
hexameter about your performance in her
fruitful and salacious heaven.

THREE

Things That Keep and Do Not Change

The man whose wife is afraid
I have fallen in love with him
asks, why do I always lie
whenever I've placed everyone in danger?
He lies naked on their unmade bed
and I place my wedding ring
on the tip of his half-erect penis

before slipping it back
onto the tip of my tongue. I do not care
why he lies. This spring I have become
obsessed with danger, my children
in the wild garden flapping
like birds his wife has attracted
to the feeder. I ask him if he will
remember this day but I know already
he has forgotten, ear cocked to something
beyond, beating back the growth.

When your left arm touched my right
as we both reached for the dessert
menu in the all-night diner, a spark
began smouldering in my sleeve, broke
a hole the size of a heart in the patched
elbow of your jacket.

Dirty white smoke enveloped our bodies
as the conversation turned
to the underground fire we'd all seen
on the news, a fire that had raged up
to consume everything in its path.
The air in the diner stank of charred meat;
under the table I took my husband's right
hand and placed it on my left thigh
where flesh and garter meet.

I wanted only that, until your left knee
grazed my right, and this time
there was an explosion, just as our waiter
lit the Crepes Suzette your wife had ordered
for you. Flames engulfed our table
and we moved to another booth, my husband
and your wife saying *we can't take
you two anywhere* simultaneously.

I had to decide: should I risk
asking for something sweet now, or abstain? –
when you said, think of the women on the *Titanic*
who pushed away from dessert that night
because their skirts were getting tight.
It made me think all right

and then when we were all friends again,
laughing, the whole length of your left leg
rubbed the length of my right and every
light in the joint went out, life stopped
for me, it meant a scandal somewhere in the future.

I tried to focus on the scorched dessert
menu feeling the beginnings of violent
pleasure. I reached for my knee where the hair
had been singed off, where the flesh was
already oozing, and I remember thinking,
I like this. It was the beginning
of loneliness, also.

For when the lights came back on I was
afraid to move from my seat; when we rose
to say goodnight we would be expected
to embrace. We had to: the flesh

of your body down the length of my trembling
body, the thin cloth covering my breasts
covered with flames, the apologies to your wife

for the plastic buttons on your shirt front melting,
your belt buckle welding us together in our heat.

At home I'm still burning when my husband
pours lighter fluid on his hands and feet and sets
himself on fire: only by entering fire can I
put the fire out. This time I might finally
do it. It may be a threat, an end to pain,
or all there is left to make of love.

EIGHT DAYS WITHOUT YOU
For Stephen

"My hands refused to serve:
My body is the house.
Each plaything that he touched, a nerve."

— Stephen Spender

You've been away a week
longer than you promised
and last night I dreamed a rapist
entered our house and I wanted him
as long as he vowed not to touch me
when it was all over. Those
were the conditions I laid
down before I let him undo
my dress and feast between my legs
using our second-best dinner service.
Next thing I knew I was comatose
and you were coming down the drive
wondering why I'd left the windows wide
open. You knew something
was wrong — I could tell by the way
you jumped from the Volkswagen while
the engine was still running, and cried
"My wife!" You'd never called me
your wife before and now you were feeling
possessive but it was too late
another man had broken his promises

to me, and a short curved knife, blunt
from so many sharpenings, filled
my new body with a kind of singing.

"... long, neon striplights twitch into life –
light spills across the pavement like a knife."

– Stephen Knight

Seven years of marriage and another
women flicks a hip at you
in a topless bar and you take her
nipples in your teeth and the next thing
I know you're sending postcards
from California telling me about
colourful migrating butterflies. I'm left
with two children who give me butterfly
kisses all night and a third who won't
weep but thinks you're up at the garage
having another breakdown. The woman
you're with doesn't own underwear,
you add – an afterthought – you hope
I'm doing great. My life, an old habit,
breaks hard.

"Where does everything go when it comes in?
What should I do with the pure speech of cells
where we find ourselves?"

– Stephen Berg

Last night at the White Knight Bar
I disguised myself as everybody's wife.
All the men talked of betrayal,
how I wasn't the same woman
they'd married. I showed them flesh,
it was what they wanted to see;
outside in the parking lot I lay down
on the hood of a Dodge and waited
for the drink to take effect on me.
What can a drunk tell you
about the light around the body,
too bright to see. I was married once.
Twice, maybe. Three times, can you
credit it? I still want every man
I can't be part of, but those
with jailhouse eyes and gold
bars around their hearts
thrill me most.

"Madness may well
be a crowded mind. But fury comes to the
stripped life."
                                        — Stephen Sandy

You've been gone so long
I've forgotten how to love
myself, it's almost as if
hunger is teaching me a lesson
about the ways of the flesh.
I'm some wild woman. I spent years
locked in the bedrooms of strangers,
preparing to be loved. But I don't know
where you've been and now a man
with a shy face like my father's
shows me photographs of torturers bouncing
children on their knees. When I ask
why the children have not been mutilated
like me, he says there is something
terrible and dark in my nature.

"he would change she would follow his parabolas
against the stars defining it
in the darkness under the searchlights."

– Stephen Holden

From Nevada you send a postcard
saying you visited every whorehouse
you could find. One woman reminded you
of me; she made you come inside her mouth
thirty-three times, once for every year
of my life. Another could spray the room
with bullets from her vagina when you
nibbled her reconstructed nipples. She
wanted it rough so you made her crawl
on the floor and drool like a dog while you
entered her from behind. You tell me this
because you believe in being open

and it's wide open country out there
under a big sky hot enough to burn.

"What is charity but doing something
you don't have to do, not for yourself,
not for anybody; or maybe you do it
just for the taste of meanness in it?"

— Stephen Dobyns

You ask me to imagine the world
through your eyes and I imagine
your head at night on a fleshy pillow
and you unable to sleep because of the hard
brown nipples that seem to stretch
towards you offering nourishment and sex.

No, you say, instead you are inside this church
with a brown-eyed girl you picked up
hitchhiking out of Albuquerque who is
kneeling at your feet trying
to give you pleasure. You needed
to hear my voice and now you're getting it
up, she's taking it down
the throat, you're praying God
won't intervene in this young girl's
mouth because God knows she is deeply
religious. I imagine your suit
needs pressing around the knees. *Talk
to me*, you whisper. *Make it good for me.*

"What a needy, desperate thing
to claim what's wild for oneself . . ."

— Stephen Dunn

I've followed your journey along a road
map never losing track of the telephone
calls you make, stranded beside a highway
with a woman who claims to want butt-love
in the back seat with a mickey of bourbon
kicked back inside her. You say my needs
were easier to meet. I want to ask you
to come home next time when the call comes
from a seaside room with a pink shell motif
where you're holed up with two women who have
to be handcuffed to the kitchen sink trap
before they can experience pleasure.
They smelled strong after six days on the road
and no bath. When you reached the coast
you asked them to undress, then made them
undress you and say the word *holy* over
and over. Nothing was turning you on
any more, you said, and now you'd lost
their keys, you were checking out, tired
of trying to forget me. I take off
my wedding ring thinking of the lights
going off all over town. Out on the fire
escape a woman sings to a man
who has left her without anything.

"The warm rain fell in fierce showers and ceased and fell.
Pretty soon you got used to its always being that way."

— Stephen Vincent Benét

I turn off the lights and then
our young daughters wake and cry
out to me. You begin to explain:
you're home to stay, but I am listening

only to the rain, getting used to it again.

His leaving is like my heartbeat, only
temporary. We love and part and love
again until a day when grief strips me
with his eyes and takes another lover.
She is flexible, like death; she peels
off her dress to show me his unlisted
cellular telephone numbers tattooed
across her breasts. Grief takes her

on his knee. She begins to breathe as he
licks her nipples, brown and big,
then bites down hard onto those faded
tattoos around her areolas.

When he comes back to me I will not ask –
what *about* those tattoos around her areolas?
It would be awkward, speaking of love
and its subsidiaries, this hurt
so fierce it would take more than all
our human grief to beat a way back through it.

Across the bay, lightning. I had wanted
to be small rain on your face, no heavier
than a human tear. When you walk in
out of that storm how easy it would be
to say, touch me. How trusting
you look. How I brush back my hair.

That morning I returned to beg for pesos
or scraps of pork scratchings
out of the fat hands of a man
I thought would remember.

The way he looked at me it was as if
a knife had nicked off the part of me
that could still gather up love
into its stillness.

Later in the day when I walked past
his table for the last time, the slant of light
on his face had made that fire seem colder,
the way, in certain light, gold changes

and the child on my back began to grow
heavier than the one unborn, still,
inside me. I felt naked like a woman
who's just walked over her own grave
and felt her bones rising
to cradle her in the truest way.

And I would have turned away
like the feral cats, the strays
who compete for the considerations
of no one, but I didn't, I stayed,
knowing he would have to explain

my presence to his good friend, the one
he'd shared me with on a hard table
in a room off the Avenida Sexta less
than twelve hours ago. The two men drank

to the women they would love, under
the bodies of the machine-gun crew slung
over the balcony above. They sat that way,
a rifle between them, neither one making
the first move to remember.

They had gathered in a field, the wild
woman they called witch strapped to a fence-post,
stripped but for her snow boots of rabbit
and a lemon-coloured scarf. They lit a fire
and watched her burn as their children
poked the meat off her body with sticks.

The men called to me, to warm myself
at her fire; one placed his ox-hide
overcoat on my shoulders, his gloves
of heavy sealskin on my hands. My mother's
eyes told me to be grateful, I had youth,
I had it all. She must have believed I even had
her man, who slipped his hands inside the overcoat
and caressed me as if he had been aroused
by her pain, and the fire nourished him.

Years later I could see my mother's eyes every time
I took a wedge of lemon between my teeth and sucked
the bitterness dry. I felt her scarf tugging at me
as her voice carried high into the star-pitched sky.
The old man who had once been her young lover
said he'd always believed a warm woman was god

as he'd entered me that night. Even where I burned
he still felt the desire to praise her.

You walk into the white field, squat
between rows of frozen cabbages, almost happy
he is gone. You spread the money all around you
on the ground, remembering how it felt
when he put it in your hands.

If You Dream of Finding Hairpins
of a Rival Woman:

you are being deceived by your mate
or maybe you are deceiving him and you
don't know it. Either way the dream is
undeniable, like a reversible scarf caught
in the spokes of a speeding convertible.
You once knew two sisters who died and had
their bodies laid to rest under a shag
carpet. People stepped on them, the dog
slept on them, but their red hair kept growing
up through the rug. It lay humped
across the rug like old roadkills
while their relatives tried backcombing
the life back into it. This reminds you
of the hospital where families of people
in comas brush and keep brushing, hoping
the comatose can tell. You sing *only*
the comatose until someone tells you
to shut up. She whispers that you should
kill yourself, but he's not worth that
much. You take the hairpins he has
arranged on your pillow and rearrange
them into the shape of an erect penis, bigger
than one he ever dreamed of. Oh, what's this?
he might say, when he comes to bed wearing

a lampshade over his head to keep his
Mohawk from being flattened. Hairpins
you might reply. But you hear the question
in your own voice and think of Osiris
dying without issue, and Isis warming
his body with her hair until his heart
turned over and his penis moved and how she
worked him over all night drawing his essence
out of him, all the time sweating only slightly
at the roots of her dutifully combed hair.

If You Dream of Hair Growing
from the Edges of Your Mouth:

sudden death. You came close the day
he threatened to toss you by your dark roots
from the garage roof because his boiled
egg was overcooked, and you inscribed
on the white bits floating in the cracked
bowl like beluga flesh *to live*
in the hearts of those we love
is never to die.

When you gave him your heart he poked it
full of hairpins like an onion studded
with cloves ready to be stuffed in the roasting
pan next to a holiday turkey. So much for love
and its subsidiaries. You learned about death
suddenly one Sunday as you sat slumped
at the hairdressers and realized the red
sheet they covered you with, to keep the cut
hair from getting under your skin, had been
placed over your head, also.

If You Dream of Eating Hair:

joy. Take your folding chair
outside and soak your feet in a bowl
filled with lavender flower water
and thyme. Let the strands
of your loose hair floss your clacking
teeth, loosen your Oriental robe and
flash your breasts at passing motorists.
Who gives a shit? your son says
pouring a bottle of your best Scotch
on the sunflowers you had been
purposefully cultivating. Your daughter
is licking a dog's face, throwing up
her blanket picturing Vincent van Gogh;
hair's an eighth of an inch
from the brain, she says. You let down
your own and mix it with the flour,
shortening, the two eggs, pinch of nutmeg,
dash of cloves. The dog moves
from your daughter's bed, sniffs
the batter, and coughs up red
hairpins.

If You Dream of the Short Hair
of Prisoners:

expect pregnancy in the future.
If he is born pointing a gun, teach him
the word for nakedness in all languages.
Don't mention red underwear. If he refuses
your milk teach him to decipher inkblots,
to say *terrorist* without stuttering.
Let him learn to break
out of handcuffs using bent hairpins,
retch like a dog. Take him
to the graveyard every Sunday and make him
fuck the earth until he can spell the word
love without cheating.

If You Dream of Being Bald:

you will find yourself disbarred
from the society of refined people.
You are likely to indulge in vices
that would make your mother's milk
curdle. You have a penchant for fat
women whose labia are held together
with hairpins. You like to squat
over mirrors in which tumulus clouds
are reflected and defecate in the middle
of thunderclaps. Your wife wears lavender
perfume behind her ears, but you lost
your sense of smell on a southbound train
in Italy during the war. Someone was playing
a violin all night up and down the corridor,
a man with a toupee was caressing a dog
with a widow's peak and a woman with wings
bumped into you, excused herself and then
said meet me tomorrow in the graveyard, but you
never did. You have red hair on the palms
of your hands and the tattoo of a faded kiss
under your left nipple, which you had pierced
at Amo's Tattoo Parlour in Toronto
on a bender. If anyone asks you the significance
of the kiss, *it's a joke*, you always tell them
but more often than not when you wake up
no one is laughing.

If You Dream of Being Covered With Hair:

you will become a voluptuous person.
You will eat nothing but sweet butter,
or rub it in all your orifices for good
luck and protection. You will take the dog
for long walks in the mirror and make him
sit for hours while you try to paint
his maligned expression. Milk is what
you will drink on Sundays, and the porcelain
dolls with no eyes you have your daughter
lay out on the bed for you have hair
the colour of spilled moonlight. You lift
their dresses over their heads because
the glare from their skin makes you
impotent. Between her legs one has
a graveyard, one a mirror, and one a dog
whose erection is studded with hairpins.
You can't decide which doll is
for you until your wife comes in
and lifts her red dress up over her head
and the room is filled with the fragrance
of charred lavender.

If You Dream of Finding a Hair
When Cutting Butter, and It Doesn't
Disgust You:

unhappiness is in store. You write
the word Sunday on the back of your hand
because it reminds you of the day
you were gang-raped in a graveyard
and your friends were envious, "at least
you're getting it." But you didn't
enjoy all those drunk amateurs and besides
they disturbed your hair. When they lifted
your dress over your head you kept repeating
lavender, milk, hairpins until one of the red
faced boys said you were crazy, like a dog,
and that made them wilder because they thought
it meant you wouldn't remember
anything they did. But you remember

they used butter on their peckers
and you remember they way they divided the pound
precisely in two pieces, as if an extra inch
either way would make a mockery of symmetry.
They lacked imagination, thinking a person
could be violated only in two places, and you
remember the knife, too, how the butter
was hard and the knife got stuck in it,
how the knife kept on sticking in it
when those boys went on forcing it.

If You Dream of Having Someone
Else's Hair:

danger is imminent. If you dream
of having someone else's
red hair in a graveyard where you find
hairpins of a rival woman sticking
in the butter, throw the dog out
with the lavender water. Remember,
there's no way of looking bad
hair hasn't tried. Think of the split
ends, thin spots, cowlicks, the wandering
parts, the stray leads and the *loss*
and then ask your stylist about
the remnants of a shag carpet on sale
across the street. In the mirror
your hair spills over your shoulders
like boiled milk. You have grown tired
just brushing the hair out of your eyes
the way women do yet it's Sunday
and the smell of his Wildroot has the dog
heaving sick, makes you think of love.

In a dream you were being trampled
by miniature horses and I couldn't
save you. Their sharp hooves had cut
grooves into your delicate features
so that when you turned to me your face
had become a blaze of highways and I followed
your eyes bleeding like red tail-lights
over the ruts of our histories.

You woke up weeping because I couldn't see
the significance of this; I believe
no dream explains everything, it's incomplete
as any two people passing an accident scene
in the middle of a highway. But what do I know
about dreams, what do I remember
of my own except driving out of

control, sun in my eyes, offering
you a pair of red sunglasses, the lenses
smashed out. No thanks, you said, preferring
to stare in your own nakedness at the sun
as if trying to discover what lies beyond
perfect vision, and so grow blind.

when the door won't open and you know
inside is the person you've been waiting
to discover, like a love letter
addressed in familiar handwriting,
postmarked from a foreign country.

But the padlock has rusted shut
and won't come undone, not even when
you hit it with the skull-shaped rock
you dug up on the beach as the tide
changed and the gulls rasped like dry hinges
in a swinging door, no it isn't going to open

to reveal what you've been longing for
and what can you do but change your style
of weeping? It hits you, hard, and your heart
shrivels into a fist, it wants to knock
the dazed look off the day's face

as the man who plans to leave you
walks towards you over the tender grass
and frees the rusty padlock with a gentle
twist, as if all he ever needed was to be
coaxed, encouraged, praised.

But you were too afraid.
And love has left you alone in this
place, reaching for a way.

After a week of rough seas the ship docked
at Hopedale. The weather was no good but still
I struggled ashore and climbed to the desecrated
churchyard, determined to take away something
of a memory, to photograph the white Arctic
poppies. Each time I framed a shot, my hands
steady at last, a hunchback on crutches teetered
into sight, as if innocently waiting for the fog
to lift, the rain to let up, the light
to throw open its dingy overcoat and expose
itself to my nakedness. My eye, my whole body
had been saving itself for this, but every time
he humped into view, I thought of you, the best
man I'd ever left, lips tasting of whatever you'd had
to eat: spicy eggplant baba ghanouj, jumbo
shrimp in garlic and Chablis, your mother's
meat pie with a dash of cinnamon
and cloves. When the sun broke

through I'd have those wildflowers posed,
I'd be poised to shoot, and then the stooped
shadow would fall as if to say beauty
without imperfection was something to be
ashamed of, as if he could be my flaw.
Crouched beside an abandoned grave
I tried to focus on those white
poppies in light that went on failing,

seeing your perfect body in his
crippled gaze. I could have taken him

back to my cabin aboard the ship, laid
his crutches down, bathed him, bent over
his grateful body and licked the smell
of smoked trout and caribou hide from his
thighs. Perhaps this is what he hoped for,
and then to be called beautiful afterwards.

I took his photograph. He'd wanted that too
and suddenly I felt blessed, I felt
I'd been taken the way I liked it best: sex

In the head on sacred ground that has been
roughed up a little, a graveyard full
of ghostly poppies choking out the dead.

Out on the windy gulf, breakers
like bouldery sheets of laundry
tumble and spin towards the horizon
in my sleep. We've been fogbound for three days
and I've learned the difference between bad
ice and good, how to travel in a blizzard
using the wind to set your course.

One night I woke and a white shadow
was trying to get into bed with me.
My tongue went numb and the only words
I could remember came out cold. I used to think
white was no colour at all, only your absence
making itself known, your ghost
doubling back to pull down my stiff
winter underwear from our drooping clothesline –
little thief! When they found you
the foam on the beach after the north wind
blew all night was white and deep.
We've been fogbound for days
and I've learned to set my course on the wind.

ACKNOWLEDGEMENTS

Some of these poems have appeared in the following magazines and anthologies:

An Album for Arlene (Hawthorne); *Arc*; *Border Crossings*; *Border Lines*; *B.C. Studies*; *Carnival: A Scream in High Park Reader*; *Event*; *Exile*; *Grain*; *The Malahat Review*; *Nimrod*; *Prairie Schooner*; *Qu'est-ce que la Poesie?* (Editions Jean Michael Place, Ville de Saint-Denis, Paris); *Saltwater Poetry Anthology, 1997*; *Saturday Night*; *Sub-Terrain Magazine*; *The Best American Poetry 1995* ("Exchange of Fire"); *Toronto Star*; *Vancouver Sun*.

"The Noise a Skeleton Makes Trying on a New Body," "Mute Swans," "The Laughter in the Kitchen," "Arctic Poppies," "The Moment," "The River," under the title "The Gold Luck of Carp," and "Becoming" won the 1996 CBC/Tilden Award for Poetry, and were broadcast on the CBC.

"The Moment" was selected as an Editor's Choice in *Arc*'s 2nd Annual Poem of the Year Contest, 1997.

"The Situation in Which We Are Both Amateurs" was published as a broadside in memory of William Martin Hoffer by Lazara Press in an edition of 336 copies, 300 of which are numbered, and 26 of which are lettered, and signed, for private distribution, in 1998.

89

"Desireless: Tom York (1940–1988)" was published as a broadside in memory of Thomas York, in an edition of 100 copies, by Slug Press, in 1988.

The line "Things that keep and do not change" is from the poem "Silver River" by Brigit Pegeen Kelly.

"Becoming: *Essay on Man*": The lines in italics are from Alexander Pope's *Essay on Man*. I found these lines quoted in an article in a health magazine in Labrador on a freighter. The lines weren't attributed, but I was reading the poem on Hornby Island a couple of summers ago and asked if anybody knew where they came from. A woman in the audience said, "Pope. His *Essay on Man*."

The poem "A Violation," referred to in "Becoming: *Essay on Man*," is by Richard Jackson.

The poem titles in the sequence "The Selected Poems of Paul Durcan" were inspired by the chapter headings in *Louisiana Power and Light*, a novel by John Dufresne.

Many thanks to my editor, Donna Bennett, to Peter Buck for his fine-tuning and Anita Chong for tracking down permissions, and to Clark Abbott for being the friend who wrote to thank me for Chinese willow used in the art of Japanese flower arranging, and to Aaltje Ottens: beauty here, beauty there.

* * *

The line "Things that keep and do not change" is an excerpt from the poem "Silver Lake," from *Song* by Brigit Pegeen Kelly, published by BOA Editions, Ltd., 260 East Ave., Rochester, NY 14604. Copyright © 1995 by Brigit Pegeen Kelly. Reprinted by permission of the publisher.

The quotation on page 57 is from the poem "Empty House," from *Collected Poems, 1928-1985* by Stephen Spender, published by Faber and Faber Limited, London. Reprinted by permission of the publisher.

The quotation on page 59 is from the poem "The Body Parts Launderette," from *Flowering Limbs* by Stephen Knight, published by Bloodaxe Books, Newcastle upon Tyne. Copyright © 1993 by Stephen Knight. Reprinted by permission of the publisher.

The quotation on page 60 is from the poem "The Holes," from *New and Selected Poems* by Stephen Berg, published by Copper Canyon Press, P.O. Box 271, Port Townsend, WA 98368. Copyright © 1992 by Stephen Berg. Reprinted by permission of the publisher.

The quotation on page 61 is from the poem "Et Quid Amabo Nisi Quod Aenigma Est," from *The Thread: New and Selected Poems* by Stephen Sandy, published by Louisiana State University Press. Copyright © 1998 by Stephen Sandy. Reprinted by permission of the author.

The quotation on page 62 is from the poem "In Praise of Antonioni" by Stephen Holden, found in *The New Yorker Book of Poems* (New York: Viking Press, 1969).

The quotation on page 63 is from the poem "Charity," from *Cemetery Nights* by Stephen Dobyns, published by Viking Penguin, a division of Penguin Putnam Inc. Copyright © 1987 by Stephen Dobyns. Reprinted by permission of the publisher.

The quotation on page 64 is from the poem "Hawk," from *Between Angels* by Stephen Dunn, published by W.W. Norton & Company,